KRYPTO

The SUPERDOG

SUPERMAN CREATED BY
JERRY SIEGEL AND JOE SHUSTER
BY SPECIAL ARRANGEMENT WITH
THE JERRY SIEGEL FAMILY

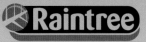

Raintree is an imprint of Capstone Global Library Limited, a company incorporated in England and Wales having its registered office at 7 Pilgrim Street, London, EC4V 6LB – Registered company number: 6695582

First published by Raintree in 2014
The moral rights of the proprietor have been asserted.

Originally published by DC Comics in the US in single magazine form as Krypto The Superdog #4.

Ashley C. Andersen Zantop Publisher
Michael Dahl Editorial Director
Donald Lemke & Sean Tulien Editors
Bob Lentz Art Director
Hilary Wacholz Designer

DC COMICS
Kristy Quinn Original US Editor

ISBN 978 1 406 27953 5

Printed in China by Nordica.
1013/CA21301918
17 16 15 14 13
10 9 8 7 6 5 4 3 2 1

British Library Cataloguing in Publication Data
A full catalogue record for this book is available from the British Library.

KRYPTO
The SUPERDOG ™

The Purr-fect Crime

JESSE LEON MCCANN..................................WRITER

MIN S. KU ....PENCILLER

JEFF ALBRECHT ....INKER

DAVE TANGUAY ....COLOURIST

DAVE TANGUAY ....LETTERER

Citrus Moi

THE PURR-FECT CRIME

JESSE LEON MCCANN: Writer • MIN S. KU: Penciller
JEFF ALBRECHT: Inker • DAVE TANGUAY: Letterer/Colorist
RACHEL GLUCKSTERN: Assoc. Editor • JOAN HILTY: Editor

THERE'S SOMETHING IN THE AIR TONIGHT. I CAN **SMELL** IT.

SNIFF, SNIFF! SMELLS LIKE **TROUBLE**.

Ji's deli

MOTEL

WHEW! THAT WAS CLOSE!

I'VE GOT TO STOP USING SUCH **EXOTIC** PURR-FUME!

8

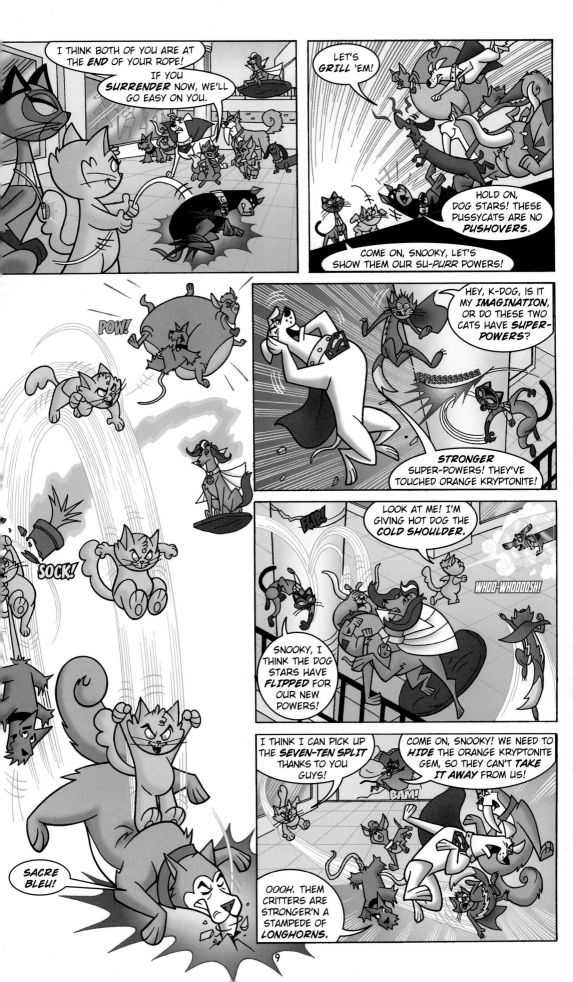

11

WAIT A MINUTE. THIS *ISN'T* THE ORANGE KRYPTONITE GEM.

GASP! SNOOKY WOOKUMS *DOUBLE-CROSSED* ME!

MEANWHILE, SNOOKY HAS TWENTY-FOUR *MORE* SUPER-POWER HOURS...

YOUR *PLAN* WORKED BRILLIANTLY, MECHANIKAT! I HAVE THE ORANGE KRYPTONITE AND A POD FULL OF *STOLEN LOOT*.

EXCELLENT, SNOOKY! RETURN TO MY SHIP AT ONCE.

I *WILL*, YOUR DOMINEERING-NESS!

OH, NO, YOU *WON'T!*

ISIS!

ARRRGH! THIS SHIP WON'T *START!* WHAT DID YOU *DO?*

CLICK-CLICK-CLICK!

WHY DO YOU LOOK SO *PURR-PLEXED?* WHEN I *VISITED* YOUR POD EARLIER, I TOOK *THIS* PRETTY *BAUBLE.*

GIVE IT BACK!

I DON'T *THINK* SO.

AND, THANKS TO [IS]IS'S *DISTRACTION*, [I]'VE GOT THE ORANGE KRYPTONITE NECKLACE.

HEY!

THAT'S NOT *FAIR!*

MIGHT AS WELL *GIVE UP*, GUV'NOR!

UNLESS YOU WANT TO *FIGHT* US...AFTER WE'VE *ALL* TOUCHED THE ORANGE KRYPTONITE AND ARE AS *POWERFUL* AS YOU.

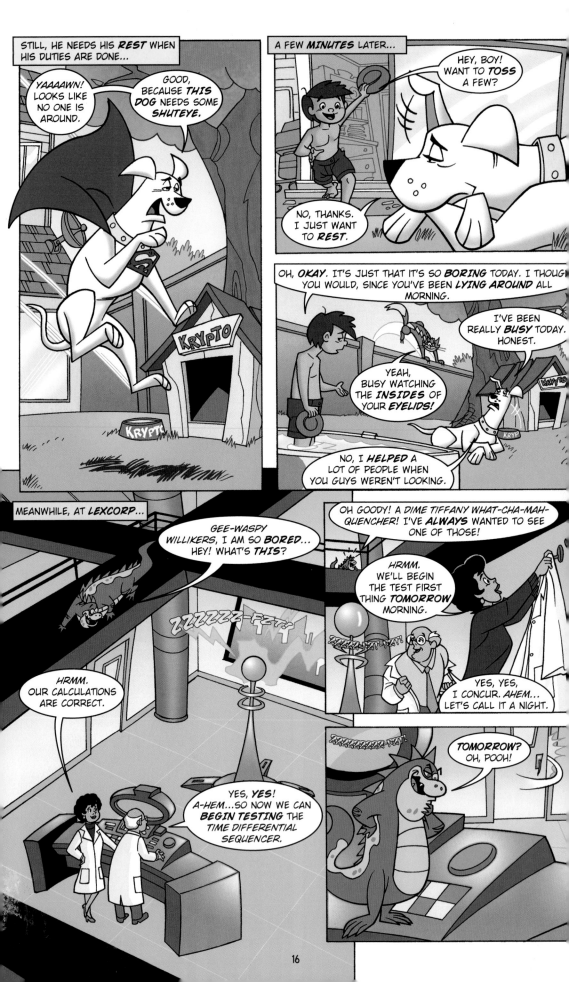

STILL, HE NEEDS HIS **REST** WHEN HIS DUTIES ARE DONE...

YAAAAWN! LOOKS LIKE NO ONE IS AROUND.

GOOD, BECAUSE **THIS DOG** NEEDS SOME **SHUTEYE.**

KRYPTO

KRYPTO

A FEW **MINUTES** LATER...

HEY, BOY! WANT TO **TOSS** A FEW?

NO, THANKS. I JUST WANT TO **REST.**

OH, **OKAY.** IT'S JUST THAT IT'S SO **BORING** TODAY. I THOUG... YOU WOULD, SINCE YOU'VE BEEN **LYING AROUND** ALL MORNING.

I'VE BEEN REALLY **BUSY** TODAY. HONEST.

YEAH, BUSY WATCHING THE **INSIDES** OF YOUR **EYELIDS!**

NO, I **HELPED** A LOT OF PEOPLE WHEN YOU GUYS WEREN'T LOOKING.

KRYP...

MEANWHILE, AT **LEXCORP...**

GEE-WASPY WILLIKERS, I AM SO **BORED...** HEY! WHAT'S **THIS?**

ZZZZZZ-FZT?!

HRMM. OUR CALCULATIONS ARE CORRECT.

YES, **YES!** A-HEM...SO NOW WE CAN **BEGIN TESTING** THE **TIME DIFFERENTIAL SEQUENCER.**

OH GOODY! A DIME TIFFANY WHAT-CHA-MAH-QUENCHER! I'VE **ALWAYS** WANTED TO SEE ONE OF THOSE!

HRMM. WE'LL BEGIN THE TEST FIRST THING **TOMORROW** MORNING.

YES, YES, I CONCUR. AHEM... LET'S CALL IT A NIGHT.

TOMORROW? OH, POOH!

16

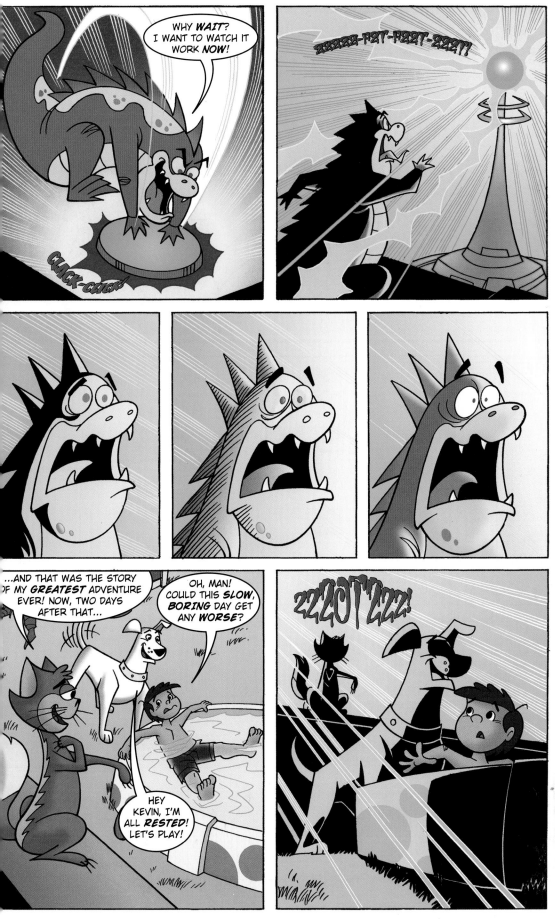

18

19

Superdog Jokes!

WHY DID THE POLICE OFFICER FINE THE PREGNANT DOG?

SHE WAS LITTERING!

WHAT HAPPENED TO THE CAT THAT SWALLOWED A BALL OF WOOL?

SHE HAD MITTENS!

WHAT DO YOU CALL A KITTEN BORN IN THE TENTH MONTH OF THE YEAR?

AN OCTO-PUSS!

WHAT DO DOGS CALL COMMAS?

A-PAW-STROPHES!

Creators

JESSE LEON MCCANN WRITER

Jesse Leon McCann is a *New York Times* Top-Ten Children's Book Writer, as well as a prolific all-ages comics writer. His credits include Pinky and the Brain, Animaniacs, and Looney Tunes for DC Comics; Scooby-Doo and Shrek 2 for Scholastic; and The Simpsons and Futurama for Bongo Comics. He lives in Los Angeles with his wife and four cats.

MIN SUNG KU PENCILLER

As a young child, Min Sung Ku dreamt of becoming a comic book illustrator. At six years old, he drew a picture of Superman standing behind the American flag. He has since achieved his childhood dream, having illustrated popular licensed comics properties such as the Justice League, Batman Beyond, Spider-Man, Ben 10, Phineas & Ferb, the Replacements, the Proud Family, Krypto the Superdog, and, of course, Superman. Min lives with his lovely wife and their beautiful twin daughters, Elisia and Eliana.

DAVE TANGUAY COLOURIST/LETTERER

David Tanguay has over 20 years of experience in the comic book industry. He has worked as an editor, layout artist, colourist, and letterer. He has also done web design, and he taught computer graphics at the State University of New York.

Glossary

ANOMALY deviation from a common rule

CONCUR agree

EXOTIC strange and fascinating, or from an unfamiliar place

FELONIOUS wicked, evil, or villainous

HARMLESS without the power or desire to do harm

ORBIT to travel around a planet, sun, or other object

SOUVENIR object that you keep to remind you of a place, person, or event

SUBTLE faint, delicate, gentle, clever, or disguised

THWARTED prevented something from happening or stopped someone from succeeding

Visual Questions & Prompts

1. IF YOU COULD MOVE AS FAST AS THE FLASH, WHAT WOULD YOU DO WITH YOUR NEWFOUND SPEED?

2. IN THIS PANEL, ISIS IS COLOURED LIKE A SHADOW. WHY DO YOU THINK THE CREATORS DECIDED TO SHOW HER THIS WAY HERE?

3. UNLIKE KRYPTO, ACE THE BAT-HOUND DOESN'T USUALLY HAVE SUPERPOWERS. WHAT OTHER KINDS OF SKILLS DOES ACE HAVE THAT HELP HIM FIGHT CRIME?

IT LOOKS LIKE SNOOKY HAS A *NEW* PARTNER IN CRIME!

JUDGING BY THE SCENT OF *FRENCH PERFUME* AND THE SUBTLE *AUBURN TINTING* ON THIS CAT HAIR, I WOULD SAY IT BELONGS TO *ISIS*, THE FELINE FEMME FATALE WHO WORKS WITH *CATWOMAN.*

3

4. IN YOUR OWN WORDS, DESCRIBE THE SEQUENCE OF EVENTS IN THIS PANEL. WHERE DOES SNOOKY WOOKUMS START, WHERE DOES HE END UP, AND HOW DOES HE GET THERE?

POW!

SOCK!

SACRE BLEU!

4